THE AGE OF REASON
Part I

The Library of Liberal Arts
OSKAR PIEST, FOUNDER

THE
AGE OF REASON
Part I

THOMAS PAINE

Edited, with an introduction, by
ALBUREY CASTELL

The Library of Liberal Arts
published by

Bobbs-Merrill Educational Publishing
Indianapolis

Thomas Paine: 1737 - 1809

THE AGE OF REASON, Part I, was originally published in 1794

. . . .

The Bobbs-Merrill Company, Inc.
4300 West 62nd Street
Indianapolis, Indiana 46268

Second (Revised) Edition
Nineteenth printing—1983

ISBN 0–672–60167–2 (pbk.)

CONTENTS

· · · · · · · · · · · · · · · · ·

THE AGE OF REASON

THOMAS PAINE: A CHRONOLOGY

1737, born, Thetford, England

1756-64, staymaker, London and elsewhere

1764-73, excise officer, London and elsewhere

1774, moved to America, having letter of introduction from Franklin

1776, *Common Sense,* in support of American War of Independence

1776-83, *American Crisis;* 16 essays, containing same support

1781, negotiated a loan from France for the United States

1784, much honored in America for his part in the War for Independence

1787-1802, in England and France

1789, presented with key to Bastille by Lafayette

1790, Burke, *Reflections on the Revolution in France*

1791, *Rights of Man,* Part I, in reply to Burke

1792, *Rights of Man,* Part II—made citizen by French government—elected to French government by city of Calais —tried in absentia and found guilty of treason by British government

1793-94, imprisoned by French government for ten months

1794, *Age of Reason,* Part I

1795, *Age of Reason,* Part II

1796, Watson, Bishop of Landaff, *The Reply to Paine; or an Apology for the Bible*

1797, founded the Church of Theophilanthropy in Paris

1802, returned to America

1809, died, New Rochelle, N. Y.

1819, bones removed to England by William Cobbett

INTRODUCTION

The Age of Reason, Part One, is a perennial minor classic in the history of theology in the modern world. There is no other book just like it, and it is doubtful that there ever will be: the times and the man were propitious in ways that have not recurred. The book addresses itself vigorously, if not bluntly, to the proposition: "It is only by the use of reason that man can discover God." It is therefore an essay in rational theology, since it proposes reason as the capacity which the theologian shall use. It is also an essay in natural theology, since it proposes nature as the datum upon which the theologian shall reason. These are, for a reader who shares its presuppositions, its constructive aspects. No reader of modern philosophical theology has cut his eyeteeth until he has read and reflected upon this stormy little book or its equivalent, nor gone far in such studies if he has remained fixed, or transfixed, in its pages.

In a manner of speaking, the *Age of Reason* has had a tin can tied to its tail since it was published in 1794. It has been smeared with the reproach of atheism. It would be difficult to suggest a more absurd designation. There is not a line of atheism in the book. Theodore Roosevelt's reference to Thomas Paine as a "filthy little atheist" is about as percipient an observation as Paine's own reference to Jesus as a "virtuous and amiable man." There is some irony, and perhaps some poetic justice, in the fact that "Tom" Paine should be indebted to "Teddy" Roosevelt for so inept a characterization. Paine's intention in writing the book was to save his contemporaries from atheism. Nothing could be more explicit than his two statements of this point. The first statement occurs in the second paragraph of his book: "The circumstance that has now taken place in France of the total abolition of the whole national order of priesthood, and of everything appertaining to compulsive systems of religion

... has ... rendered a work of this kind exceedingly necessary, lest ... we lose sight of morality, of humanity, and of the theology that is true." The second occurs in a letter to Samuel Adams: "The people of France were running headlong into atheism, and I had the work translated into their own language to stop them in that career, and fix them to the first article of everyman's creed who has any creed at all, and that first article should be—I believe in God." It might be argued that Paine's success in saving the people of France from running headlong into atheism was not as great as he would have wished; but that is another matter and no justification for theological name-calling. William Cobbett, once he had straightened out his ideas on Paine's political views, had the graciousness to come to this country, as on a pilgrimage, and carry the bones of Tom Paine back to England. An English theologian could, with equal propriety, have done the same.

The Age of Reason contains two things: first, a statement of what the author believes about God and religion and his reasons for those beliefs. As already indicated, this is rational or natural theology; secondly, a criticism of beliefs about God and religion which go beyond the author's rational or natural theology. It is as though Paine were to say: "Give me my capacity to reason, and nature upon which to exercise my reason, and I will work out a theology," and then were to add, "and anything which I cannot so obtain, I will exclude from my theology." It was, of course, these criticisms and rejections, and particularly the manner of their statement, that alienated orthodox readers and led to the charge of "atheism." These are, for the reader who shares the book's presuppositions, its destructive aspects. They constitute a criticism of those elements in eighteenth-century orthodoxy which went beyond eighteenth-century deism. Then as now, in theology as in other matters, orthodoxy resents the suggestion that it is not, in all respects, entirely rational.

The Age of Reason was written and published under colorful circumstances. Between 1776 and 1784 Paine had earned high honors in the American War for Independence. In this con-

nection he had written *Common Sense* and the papers called
American Crisis. He had been materially rewarded by grants
of land and money by Congress and by New York and Penn-
sylvania. In 1787 he went to England and France to see if he
could find backers for his idea for a single-span iron bridge.
He was thus on hand when the French Revolution began in
1789. From 1789 to 1792 he stood well with the moderate
leaders of the revolution. Lafayette presented him with the dis-
carded key of the Bastille. He was made a citizen of France.
He was elected to the revolutionary assembly, as member from
Calais. He wrote his *Rights of Man* in answer to Edmund
Burke's powerful criticism of the actions and policies of the
French revolutionary assembly. He participated in drafting the
constitution and in debates on domestic policy. However, beginning in 1792, the control of the Revolution passed into the
hands of extremists. Paine opposed this group and found himself marked for political imprisonment and execution. He was
arrested in December, 1793. In the six weeks preceding, with
the shadow of these coming events athwart him, he wrote Part
One of the *Age of Reason*. It was to be his last testament to mankind, and to deal with final things. He was arrested at 3 o'clock
in the morning. At his request he was taken, en route to the
jail, to call on his friend Joel Barlow, the American writer. To
him he entrusted the manuscript of the book. He remained in
prison for slightly over ten months. During these months the
Age of Reason, Part One, was published, carrying a dedication
to "my fellow citizens of the United States of America"; and
Part Two was written. By the end of these months the extremists
had lost control of the Revolution and Paine was released from
prison. He proceeded to publish Part Two of his *Age of Reason*.
It is safe to say of the *Age of Reason* what you can say of Paine's
two political tracts, *Common Sense* and *Rights of Man*, that it
was more widely read than any similar writing published during the last quarter of the eighteenth century.

The *Age of Reason* has been criticized and castigated since
the day it went on sale. The key sentence in the book ("It is
only by the exercise of reason that man can discover God")

indicates the two lines along which these objections have proceeded. Confronted with that key sentence, readers have made objections which may be grouped as follows: (1) They have objected to Paine's restriction of all theology to what he could arrive at in the way of rational or natural theology. They want more than a rational or natural theology. They have objected to his word "only": reason is not the only resource at man's disposal in the discovery of God; nor, in these matters, is nature reason's only datum. They do not object to either reason or nature; but they want access to something more than either; and they do not want to be ridiculed and criticized for so desiring. (2) They have objected to Paine's claim that reason can discover God. In this group are to be found the skeptics and atheists, who deny that man can discover God by the use of reason or anything else; and those elusive theologians who insist that man can discover God, but *not* by the use of reason. Doubt or denial here may be directed at reason, as a human capacity, or at nature as a datum upon which reason is to be exercised. In either case the argument instantly becomes much more complicated and sophisticated than ever Thomas Paine seems to have imagined.

In writing the *Age of Reason*, especially Part One, Paine was not pioneering, nor did he think he was. His book is a piece of vigorous theological journalism intending neither originality nor completeness. He was working a tradition that went back, in England, at least to John Locke's seventeenth-century tract, *The Reasonableness of Christianity*. This tradition was known as deism, and the eighteenth had been its great century in England, on the continent, and in the American colonies. It was the manifestation, in theology, of the spirit that had by Paine's day already gained expression in the rise of the natural sciences and in republicanism in politics. What is even more to the point in drawing attention to the journalistic character of Paine's tract, is the fact that his beloved deism had already been subjected to something like a decisive criticism by David Hume in 1776 (*Dialogues Concerning Natural Religion*) and Immanuel Kant in 1793 (*Religion Within the Limits of Mere Reason*).

It is likely that Paine did not know of these writings. If that is so, he is only exercising the journalist's privilege, in philosophy, of being somewhat behind the times.

Paine's *Age of Reason,* Part One, was published early in 1794. Toward the end of 1795, he followed it with Part Two, not reprinted in this edition. It is with Paine's *Age of Reason* as with Goethe's *Faust* or with Karl Marx's *Das Kapital:* the best-known, most influential, and most perennial portion is "Part One." In Part Two, Paine set himself to make a chapter and verse examination of the text of the Old and New Testaments, seeking to document and reinforce the general claims made in Part One. The result is a veritable thicket of quotations, cross-references, and detailed arguments which make rather arid reading today. As a document in history, Tom Paine's *Age of Reason* is Part One.

                              ALBUREY CASTELL

SELECTED BIBLIOGRAPHY

On Paine's Problem in The Age of Reason

Locke, John, *The Reasonableness of Christianity* (1695).
Butler, Joseph, *The Analogy of Religion* (1736).
Hume, David, *Dialogues Concerning Natural Religion* (1779).
Allen, Ethan, *Reason the Only Oracle of Man* (1784).
Kant, Immanuel, *Religion Within the Limits of Mere Reason* (1793).

On Paine's Life and Times

Conway, M. D., *The Life of Thomas Paine,* New York, 1892.
Best, M. A., *Thomas Paine: Prophet and Martyr of Democracy,* New York, 1927.
Pearson, H., *Tom Paine, Friend of Mankind,* New York, 1937.
Smith, F., *Thomas Paine, Liberator,* New York, 1938.
Fast, Howard, *Citizen Tom Paine* (a novel), New York, 1943.
Woodward, W. E., *Tom Paine: America's Godfather,* New York, 1945.

The Argument Since Paine

Carlyle, Thomas, *Sartor Resartus.* Ed. by R. W. Emerson. Boston, 1836.
Emerson, Ralph W., *Nature.* Boston, 1836.
————, *Essays.* Boston, 1841-1844.
Royce, Josiah, *The Religious Aspects of Philosophy. A Critique of the Bases of Conduct and of Faith.* Boston, 1885.
James, William, *Varieties of Religious Experience.* New York, 1902.
Shaw, Bernard, Preface to *Back to Methusela.* New York, 1921.
Tolstoy, Leo, *What I Believe.* Translated by A. Maude, New York, 1921.
Santayana, George, *Reason in Religion.* (Vol. 3 of The Life of Reason.) New York, 1924-1927.
Freud, Sigmund, *The Future of an Illusion.* London, 1928.

THE AGE OF REASON

Being an Investigation of
True and Fabulous Theology

PART ONE

TO MY FELLOW CITIZENS OF THE UNITED STATES OF AMERICA

I PUT the following work under your protection. It contains my opinion upon religion. You will do me the justice to remember that I have always strenuously supported the right of every man to his opinion however different that opinion might be to mine. He who denies to another this right makes a slave of himself to his present opinion, because he precludes himself the right of changing it.

The most formidable weapon against errors of every kind is reason. I have never used any other, and I trust I never shall.

Your affectionate friend and fellow citizen,

THOMAS PAINE

Luxembourg (Paris), 8th Pluvôise.
Second year of the French Republic, one and indivisible,
January 27th, O. S. 1794.

THE AGE OF REASON

IT HAS BEEN MY INTENTION, for several years past, to publish my thoughts upon religion. I am well aware of the difficulties that attend the subject and, from that consideration, had reserved it to a more advanced period of life. I intended it to be the last offering I should make to my fellow citizens of all nations, and that at a time when the purity of the motive that induced me to it could not admit of a question, even by those who might disapprove the work.

The circumstance that has now taken place in France of the total abolition of the whole national order of priesthood, and of everything appertaining to compulsive systems of religion, and compulsive articles of faith, has not only precipitated my intention, but rendered a work of this kind exceedingly necessary, lest in the general wreck of superstition, of false systems of government and false theology, we lose sight of morality, of humanity, and of the theology that is true.

As several of my colleagues, and others of my fellow citizens of France, have given me the example of making their voluntary and individual profession of faith, I also will make mine; and I do this with all that sincerity and frankness with which the mind of man communicates with itself.

I believe in one God, and no more; and I hope for happiness beyond this life.

I believe in the equality of man; and I believe that religious duties consist in doing justice, loving mercy, and endeavoring to make our fellow creatures happy.

But, lest it should be supposed that I believe in many other things in addition to these, I shall, in the progress of this work, declare the things I do not believe, and my reasons for not believing them.

I do not believe in the creed professed by the Jewish church, by the Roman church, by the Greek church, by the Turkish church, by the Protestant church, nor by any church that I know of. My own mind is my own church.

All national institutions of churches, whether Jewish, Christian, or Turkish, appear to me no other than human inventions, set up to terrify and enslave mankind, and monopolize power and profit.

I do not mean by this declaration to condemn those who believe otherwise; they have the same right to their belief as I have to mine. But it is necessary to the happiness of man that he be mentally faithful to himself. Infidelity does not consist in believing or in disbelieving; it consists in professing to believe what he does not believe.

It is impossible to calculate the moral mischief, if I may so express it, that mental lying has produced in society. When a man has so far corrupted and prostituted the chastity of his mind as to subscribe his professional belief to things he does not believe, he has prepared himself for the commission of every other crime. He takes up the trade of a priest for the sake of gain, and in order to qualify himself for that trade he begins with a perjury. Can we conceive anything more destructive to morality than this?

Soon after I had published the pamphlet *Common Sense* in America, I saw the exceeding probability that a revolution in the system of government would be followed by a revolution in the system of religion. The adulterous connection of church and state, wherever it had taken place, whether Jewish, Christian, or Turkish, had so effectually prohibited, by pains and penalties, every discussion upon established creeds and upon first principles of religion that, until the system of government should be changed, those subjects could not be brought fairly and openly before the world; but that, whenever this should be done, a revolution in the system of religion would follow. Human inventions and priestcraft would be detected, and man would return to the pure, unmixed, and unadulterated belief of one God, and no more.

Every national church or religion has established itself by pretending some special mission from God, communicated to certain individuals. The Jews have their Moses; the Christians their Jesus Christ, their apostles and saints; and the Turks their Mohammed, as if the way to God was not open to every man alike.

Each of those churches show certain books which they call "revelation," or the word of God. The Jews say that their word of God was given by God to Moses, face to face; the Christians say their word of God came by divine inspiration; and the Turks say that their word of God (the Koran) was brought by an angel from heaven. Each of those churches accuse the other of unbelief; and for my part I disbelieve them all.

As it is necessary to affix right ideas to words, I will, before I proceed further into the subject, offer some observations on the word "revelation." Revelation, when applied to religion, means something communicated *immediately* from God to man.

No one will deny or dispute the power of the Almighty to make such a communication, if he pleases. But admitting, for the sake of a case, that something has been revealed to a certain person, and not revealed to any other person, it is revelation to that person only. When he tells it to a second person, a second to a third, a third to a fourth, and so on, it ceases to be a revelation to all those persons. It is revelation to the first person only, and *hearsay* to every other, and consequently they are not obliged to believe it.

It is a contradiction in terms and ideas to call anything a revelation that comes to us at second hand, either verbally or in writing. Revelation is necessarily limited to the first communication—after this, it is only an account of something which that person says was a revelation made to him; and though he may find himself obliged to believe it, it cannot be incumbent on me to believe it in the same manner, for it was not a revelation made to *me,* and I have only his word for it that it was made to him.

When Moses told the children of Israel that he received the two tables of the Commandments from the hands of God, they were not obliged to believe him, because they had no other authority for it than his telling them so; and I have no other authority for it than some historian telling me so. The Commandments carry no internal evidence of divinity with them; they contain some good moral precepts, such as any man qualified to be a lawgiver, or a legislator, could produce himself without having recourse to supernatural intervention.[1]

When I am told that the Koran was written in heaven and brought to Mohammed by an angel, the account comes too near the same kind of hearsay evidence and secondhand authority as the former. I did not see the angel myself, and therefore I have a right not to believe it.

When also I am told that a woman called the Virgin Mary said, or gave out, that she was with child without any cohabitation with a man, and that her betrothed husband, Joseph, said that an angel told him so, I have a right to believe them or not; such a circumstance required a much stronger evidence than their bare word for it; but we have not even this—for neither Joseph nor Mary wrote any such matter themselves; it is only reported by others that *they said so*—it is hearsay upon hearsay, and I do not choose to rest my belief upon such evidence.

It is, however, not difficult to account for the credit that was given to the story of Jesus Christ being the son of God. He was born when the heathen mythology had still some fashion and repute in the world, and that mythology had prepared the people for the belief of such a story. Almost all the extraordinary men that lived under the heathen mythology were reputed to be the sons of some of their gods. It was not a new thing, at that time, to believe a man to have been celestially begotten; the intercourse of gods with women was then a matter of familiar opinion. Their Jupiter, according to their accounts, had cohabited with hundreds: the story, therefore, had nothing in it either new, wonderful, or obscene; it was conformable to the opinions that then prevailed among the people called Gentiles or mythologists, and it was those people only that believed it. The Jews who had kept strictly to the belief of one God, and no

[1] It is, however, necessary to except the declaration which says that God *visits the sins of the fathers upon the children;* it is contrary to every principle of moral justice.

more, and who had always rejected the heathen mythology, never credited the story.

It is curious to observe how the theory of what is called the Christian church sprung out of the tail of the heathen mythology. A direct incorporation took place in the first instance, by making the reputed founder to be celestially begotten. The trinity of gods that then followed was no other than a reduction of the former plurality, which was about twenty or thirty thousand; the statue of Mary succeeded the statue of Diana of Ephesus; the deification of heroes changed into the canonization of saints; the mythologists had gods for everything; the Christian mythologists had saints for everything; the church became as crowded with one, as the Pantheon had been with the other, and Rome was the place of both. The Christian theory is little else than the idolatry of the ancient mythologists accommodated to the purpose of power and revenue, and it yet remains to reason and philosophy to abolish the amphibious fraud.

Nothing that is here said can apply, even with the most distant disrespect, to the real character of Jesus Christ. He was a virtuous and an amiable man. The morality that he preached and practiced was of the most benevolent kind; and though similar systems of morality had been preached by Confucius and by some of the Greek philosophers many years before, by the Quakers since, and by many good men in all ages, it has not been exceeded by any.

Jesus Christ wrote no account of himself, of his birth, parentage, or anything else; not a line of what is called the New Testament is of his own writing. The history of him is altogether the work of other people; and as to the account of his resurrection and ascension, it was the necessary counterpart to the story of his birth. His historians, having brought him into the world in a supernatural manner, were obliged to take him out again in the same manner, or the first part of the story must have fallen to the ground.

The wretched contrivance with which the latter part is told exceeds everything that went before it. The first part, that of the miraculous conception, was not a thing that admitted of publicity; and therefore the tellers of this part of the story had this advantage that, though they might not be credited, they could not be detected. They could not be expected to prove it because it was not one of those things that admitted of proof, and it was impossible that the person of whom it was told could prove it himself.

But the resurrection of a dead person from the grave, and his ascension through the air, is a thing very different, as to the evidence it admits of, to the invisible conception of a child in the womb. The resurrection and ascension, supposing them to have taken place, admitted of public and ocular demonstration, like that of the ascension of a balloon or the sun at noonday, to all Jerusalem at least. A thing which everybody is required to believe requires that the proof and evidence of it should be equal to all and universal; and as the public visibility of this last related act was the only evidence that could give sanction to the former part, the whole of it falls to the ground because that evidence never was given. Instead of this, a small number of persons, not more than eight or nine, are introduced as proxies for the whole world, to say they saw it, and all the rest of the world are called upon to believe it. But it appears that Thomas did not believe the resurrection and, as they say, would not believe without having ocular and manual demonstration himself. *So neither will I,* and the reason is equally as good for me and for every other person as for Thomas.

It is in vain to attempt to palliate or disguise this matter. The story, so far as relates to the supernatural part, has every mark of fraud and imposition stamped upon the face of it. Who were the authors of it is as impossible for us now to know, as it is for us to be assured that the books in which the account is related were written by the persons whose names they bear; the best surviving evidence we now have respecting this affair is the Jews. They are regularly descended from the people who lived in the times this resurrection and ascension is said to have happened, and they say *it is not true.* It has long appeared to me a strange inconsistency to cite the Jews as a proof of the truth of the story.

It is just the same as if a man were to say, I will prove the truth of what I have told you by producing the people who say it is false.

That such a person as Jesus Christ existed, and that he was crucified, which was the mode of execution at that day, are historical relations strictly within the limits of probability. He preached most excellent morality and the equality of man, but he preached also against the corruptions and avarice of the Jewish priests, and this brought upon him the hatred and vengeance of the whole order of priesthood. The accusation which those priests brought against him was that of sedition and conspiracy against the Roman government, to which the Jews were then subject and tributary; and it is not improbable that the Roman government might have some secret apprehensions of the effects of his doctrine, as well as the Jewish priests; neither is it improbable that Jesus Christ had in contemplation the delivery of the Jewish nation from the bondage of the Romans. Between the two, however, this virtuous reformer and revolutionist lost his life.

It is upon this plain narrative of facts, together with another case I am going to mention, that the Christian mythologists, calling themselves the Christian church, have erected their fable which, for absurdity and extravagance, is not exceeded by anything that is to be found in the mythology of the ancients.

The ancient mythologists tell us that the race of Giants made war against Jupiter, and that one of them threw a hundred rocks against him at one throw; that Jupiter defeated him with thunder, and confined him afterward under Mount Etna, and that every time the Giant turns himself Mount Etna belches fire.

It is here easy to see that the circumstance of the mountain, that of its being a volcano, suggested the idea of the fable; and that the fable is made to fit and wind itself up with that circumstance.

The Christian mythologists tell us that their Satan made war against the Almighty, who defeated him and confined him afterward, not under a mountain, but in a pit. It is here easy to see that the first fable suggested the idea of the second; for the fable of Jupiter and the Giants was told many hundred years before that of Satan.

Thus far the ancient and the Christian mythologists differ very little from each other. But the latter have contrived to carry the matter much farther. They have contrived to connect the fabulous part of the story of Jesus Christ with the fable originating from Mount Etna; and in order to make all the parts of the story tie together, they have taken to their aid the traditions of the Jews; for the Christian mythology is made up partly from the ancient mythology and partly from the Jewish traditions.

The Christian mythologists, after having confined Satan in a pit, were obliged to let him out again to bring on the sequel of the fable. He is then introduced into the Garden of Eden in the shape of a snake or a serpent, and in that shape he enters into familiar conversation with Eve, who is noway surprised to hear a snake talk; and the issue of this *tête-à-tête* is that he persuades her to eat an apple, and the eating of that apple damns all mankind.

After giving Satan this triumph over the whole creation, one would have supposed that the church mythologists would have been kind enough to send him back again to the pit; or, if they had not done this, that they would have put a mountain upon him (for they say that their faith can remove a mountain), or have put him *under* a mountain, as the former mythologists had done, to prevent him getting again among the women and doing more mischief. But instead of this they leave him at large, without even obliging him to give his parole—the secret of which is that they could not do without him; and after being at the trouble of making him, they bribed him to stay. They promised him *all* the Jews, *all* the Turks by anticipation, nine-tenths of the world besides, and Mohammed into the bargain. After this, who can doubt the bountifulness of the Christian mythology?

Having thus made an insurrection and a battle in Heaven, in which none of the combatants could be either killed or wounded —put Satan into the pit—let him out again—giving him a triumph over the whole creation—damned all mankind by the eating of an apple, these Christian mythologists bring the two ends of their fable together. They represent this virtuous and amiable man, Jesus Christ, to be at once both God and man, and also the Son of God, celestially begotten, on purpose to be sacrificed, because they say that Eve in her longing had eaten an apple.

Putting aside everything that might excite laughter by its absurdity, or detestation by its profaneness, and confining ourselves merely to an examination of the parts, it is impossible to conceive a story more derogatory to the Almighty, more inconsistent with his wisdom, more contradictory to his power than this story is.

In order to make for it a foundation to rise upon, the inventors were under the necessity of giving to the being whom they call Satan a power equally as great, if not greater, than they attribute to the Almighty. They have not only given him the power of liberating himself from the pit, after what they call his fall, but they have made that power increase afterward to infinity. Before this fall they represent him only as an angel of limited existence, as they represent the rest. After his fall, he becomes, by their account, omnipresent. He exists everywhere, and at the same time. He occupies the whole immensity of space.

Not content with this deification of Satan, they represent him as defeating, by stratagem, in the shape of an animal of the creation, all the power and wisdom of the Almighty. They represent him as having compelled the Almighty to the *direct necessity* either of surrendering the whole of the creation to the government and sovereignty of this Satan or of capitulating for its redemption by coming down upon earth and exhibiting himself upon a cross in the shape of a man.

Had the inventors of this story told it the contrary way, that is, had they represented the Almighty as compelling Satan to exhibit *himself* on a cross, in the shape of a snake, as a punishment for his new transgression, the story would have been less absurd—less contradictory. But instead of this, they make the transgressor triumph, and the Almighty fall.

That many good men have believed this strange fable and lived very good lives under that belief (for credulity is not a crime) is what I have no doubt of. In the first place, they were educated to believe it, and they would have believed anything else in the same manner. There are also many who have been so enthusiastically enraptured by what they conceived to be the infinite love of God to man, in making a sacrifice himself, that the vehemence of the idea has forbidden and deterred them from examining into the absurdity and profaneness of the story. The more unnatural anything is, the more it is capable of becoming the object of dismal admiration.

But if objects for gratitude and admiration are our desire, do they not present themselves every hour to our eyes? Do we not see a fair creation prepared to receive us the instant we are born —a world furnished to our hands that cost us nothing? Is it we that light up the sun, that pour down the rain and fill the earth with abundance? Whether we sleep or wake, the vast machinery of the universe still goes on. Are these things, and the blessings they indicate in future, nothing to us? Can our gross feelings be excited by no other subjects than tragedy and suicide? Or is the gloomy pride of man become so intolerable that nothing can flatter it but a sacrifice of the Creator?

I know that this bold investigation will alarm many, but it would be paying too great a compliment to their credulity to forbear it on their account; the times and the subject demand it to be done. The suspicion that the theory of what is called the Christian church is fabulous is becoming very extensive in all countries; and it will be a consolation to men staggering under that suspicion, and doubting what to believe and what to disbelieve, to see the object freely investigated. I therefore pass on to the examinations of the books called the Old and New Testament.

These books, beginning with Genesis and ending with Revelation (which, by the by, is a book of riddles that requires a revelation to explain it), are, we are told, the word of God. It is, therefore, proper for us to know who told us so, that we may know what credit to give to the report. The answer to this question is that nobody can tell, except that we tell one another so. The case, however, historically appears to be as follows:

When the church mythologists established their system, they collected all the writings they could find and managed them as they pleased. It is a matter altogether of uncertainty to us whether such of the writings as now appear under the name of the Old and New Testament are in the same state in which those collectors say they found them, or whether they added, altered, abridged, or dressed them up.

Be this as it may, they decided by *vote* which of the books out of the collection they had made should be the *word of God,* and which should not. They rejected several; they voted others to be doubtful, such as the books called the Apocrypha; and those books which had a majority of votes were voted to be the word of God. Had they voted otherwise, all the people, since calling themselves Christians, had believed otherwise—for the belief of the one comes from the vote of the other. Who the people were that did all this we know nothing of; they called themselves by the general name of the Church, and this is all we know of the matter.

As we have no other external evidence or authority for believing these books to be the word of God than what I have mentioned, which is no evidence or authority at all, I come, in the next place, to examine the internal evidence contained in the books themselves.

In the former part of this essay I have spoken of revelation; I now proceed further with that subject, for the purpose of applying it to the books in question.

Revelation is a communication of something which the person to whom that thing is revealed did not know before. For if I have done a thing or seen it done, it needs no revelation to tell me I have done it or seen it, nor to enable me to tell it or to write it.

Revelation, therefore, cannot be applied to anything done upon earth, of which man himself is the actor or the witness; and, consequently, all the historical and anecdotal parts of the Bible, which is almost the whole of it, is not within the meaning and compass of the word "revelation," and, therefore, is not the word of God.

When Samson ran off with the gateposts of Gaza, if he ever did so (and whether he did or not is nothing to us), or when he visited his Delilah, or caught his foxes, or did anything else, what has revelation to do with these things? If they were facts, he could tell them himself, or his secretary, if he kept one, could write them if they were worth either telling or writing; and if they were fictions, revelation could not make them true; and whether true or not, we are neither the better nor the wiser for knowing them. When we contemplate the immensity of that Being who directs and governs the incomprehensible *whole* of which the utmost ken of human sight can discover but a part, we ought to feel shame at calling such paltry stories the word of God.

As to the account of the Creation, with which the Book of Genesis opens, it has all the appearance of being a tradition which the Israelites had among them before they came into Egypt; and after their departure from that country they put it at the head of their history, without telling (as it is most probable) that they did not know how they came by it. The manner in which the account opens shows it to be traditionary. It begins abruptly; it is nobody that speaks; it is nobody that hears; it is addressed to nobody; it has neither first, second, nor third person; it has every criterion of being a tradition; it has no voucher. Moses does not take it upon himself by introducing it with the formality that he uses on other occasions, such as that of saying, "The Lord spake unto Moses, saying. . . ."

Why it has been called the Mosaic account of the Creation, I am at a loss to conceive. Moses, I believe, was too good a judge of such subjects to put his name to that account. He had been educated among the Egyptians, who were a people as well skilled in science and particularly in astronomy as any people of their day; and the silence and caution that Moses observes in not authenticating the account is a good negative evidence that he neither told it nor believed it. The case is that every nation of people has been worldmakers, and the Israelites had as much right to set up the trade of worldmaking as any of the rest; and as Moses was not an Israelite, he might not choose to contradict the tradition. The account, however, is harmless; and this is more than can be said of many other parts of the Bible.

Whenever we read the obscene stories, the voluptuous debaucheries, the cruel and torturous executions, the unrelenting vindictiveness, with which more than half the Bible is filled, it would be more consistent that we called it the word of a demon than the word of God. It is a history of wickedness that has served to corrupt and brutalize mankind; and, for my part, I sincerely detest it, as I detest everything that is cruel.

We scarcely meet with anything, a few phrases excepted, but what deserves either our abhorrence or our contempt, till we come to the miscellaneous parts of the Bible. In the anonymous publications, the Psalms and the Book of Job, more particularly in the latter, we find a great deal of elevated sentiment reverentially expressed of the power and benignity of the Almighty; but they stand on no higher rank than many other compositions on similar subjects, as well before that time as since.

The Proverbs which are said to be Solomon's, though most probably a collection (because they discover a knowledge of life which his situation excluded him from knowing), are an instructive table of ethics. They are inferior in keenness to the proverbs of the Spaniards, and not more wise and economical than those of the American Franklin.

All the remaining parts of the Bible, generally known by the name of the Prophets, are the works of the Jewish poets and itinerant preachers, who mixed poetry,[2] anecdote, and devotion

[2] As there are many readers who do not see that a composition is poetry unless it be in rhyme, it is for their information that I add this note.

Poetry consists principally in two things—imagery and composition. The composition of poetry differs from that of prose in the manner of mixing long and short syllables together. Take a long syllable out of a line of poetry and put a short one in the room of it, or put a long syllable where a short one should be, and that line will lose its poetical harmony. It will have an effect upon the line like that of misplacing a note in a song. The imagery in these books called the Prophets appertains altogether to poetry. It is fictitious and often extravagant, and not admissible in any other kind of writing than poetry. To show that these writings are composed in poetical numbers, I will take ten syllables as they stand in the book, and make a line

together—and those works still retain the air and style of poetry, though in translation.

There is not, throughout the whole book called the Bible, any word that describes to us what we call a poet, nor any word that describes what we call poetry. The case is that the word "prophet," to which latter times have affixed a new idea, was the Bible word for poet, and the word "prophesying" meant the art of making poetry. It also meant the art of playing poetry to a tune upon any instrument of music.

We read of prophesying with pipes, tabrets, and horns—of prophesying with harps, with psalteries, with cymbals, and with every other instrument of music then in fashion. Were we now to speak of prophesying with a fiddle, or with a pipe and tabor, the expression would have no meaning or would appear ridiculous, and to some people contemptuous, because we have changed the meaning of the word.

We are told of Saul being among the *prophets,* and also that he prophesied; but we are not told what *they prophesied,* nor what *he prophesied.* The case is, there was nothing to tell; for these prophets were a company of musicians and poets, and Saul joined in the concert, and this was called prophesying.

The account given of this affair in the book called Samuel is that Saul met a company of prophets; a whole company of them! coming down with a psaltery, a tabret, a pipe, and a harp, and that they prophesied, and that he prophesied with them.

---

of the same number of syllables (heroic measure) that shall rhyme with the last word. It will then be seen that the composition of these books is poetical measure. The instance I shall produce is from Isaiah:

> "*Hear, O ye heavens, and give ear, O earth!*"
> 'Tis God Himself that calls attention forth.

Another instance I shall quote is from the mournful Jeremiah, to which I shall add two other lines, for the purpose of carrying out the figure, and showing the intention of the poet:

> "*O! that mine head were waters and mine eyes*"
> Were fountains flowing like the liquid skies;
> Then would I give the mighty flood release,
> And weep a deluge for the human race.

But it appears afterward that Saul prophesied badly, that is, he performed his part badly; for it is said that an "evil spirit from God" [3] came upon Saul, and he prophesied.

Now, were there no other passage in the book called the Bible than this to demonstrate to us that we have lost the original meaning of the word "prophesy" and substituted another meaning in its place, this alone would be sufficient; for it is impossible to use and apply the word "prophesy" in the place it is here used and applied if we give to it the sense which latter times have affixed to it. The manner in which it is here used strips it of all religious meaning and shows that a man might then be a prophet, or he might "prophesy," as he may now be a poet or a musician, without any regard to the morality or immorality of his character. The word was originally a term of science, promiscuously applied to poetry and to music, and not restricted to any subject upon which poetry and music might be exercised.

Deborah and Barak are called prophets, not because they predicted anything, but because they composed the poem or song that bears their name, in celebration of an act already done. David is ranked among the prophets, for he was a musician, and was also reputed to be (though perhaps very erroneously) the author of the Psalms. But Abraham, Isaac, and Jacob are not called prophets; it does not appear from any accounts we have that they could either sing, play music, or make poetry.

We are told of the greater and the lesser prophets. They might as well tell us of the greater and the lesser God; for there cannot be degrees in prophesying consistently with its modern sense. But there are degrees in poetry, and therefore the phrase is reconcilable to the case when we understand by it the greater and the lesser poets.

It is altogether unnecessary, after this, to offer any observations upon what those men, styled prophets, have written. The axe goes at once to the root, by showing that the original mean-

[3] As those men who call themselves divines and commentators are very fond of puzzling one another, I leave them to contest the meaning of the first part of the phrase, that of *an evil spirit from God*. I keep to my text—I keep to the meaning of the word prophesy.

ing of the word has been mistaken; and, consequently, all the inferences that have been drawn from those books, the devotional respect that has been paid to them, and the labored commentaries that have been written upon them, under that mistaken meaning, are not worth disputing about. In many things, however, the writings of the Jewish poets deserve a better fate than that of being bound up, as they now are, with the trash that accompanies them, under the abused name of the word of God.

If we permit ourselves to conceive right ideas of things, we must necessarily affix the idea, not only of unchangeableness, but of the utter impossibility of any change taking place, by any means or accident whatever, in that which we would honor with the name of the word of God; and therefore the word of God cannot exist in any written or human language.

The continually progressive change to which the meaning of words is subject, the want of a universal language which renders translation necessary, the errors to which translations are again subject, the mistakes of copyists and printers, together with the possibility of willful alteration, are of themselves evidences that the human language, whether in speech or in print, cannot be the vehicle of the word of God. The word of God exists in something else.

Did the book called the Bible excel in purity of ideas and expression all the books that are now extant in the world, I would not take it for my rule of faith, as being the word of God, because the possibility would nevertheless exist of my being imposed upon. But when I see throughout the greater part of this book scarcely anything but a history of the grossest vices and a collection of the most paltry and contemptible tales, I cannot dishonor my Creator by calling it by his name.

Thus much for the Bible; I now go on to the book called the New Testament. The *New* Testament! that is, the *new* will, as if there could be two wills of the Creator.

Had it been the object or the intention of Jesus Christ to establish a new religion, he would undoubtedly have written a system himself or *procured it to be written* in his lifetime. But

there is no publication extant authenticated with his name. All
the books called the New Testament were written after his
death. He was a Jew by birth and by profession; and he was the
son of God in like manner that every other person is—for the
Creator is the Father of *all*.

The first four books, called Matthew, Mark, Luke, and John,
do not give a history of the life of Jesus Christ, but only detached
anecdotes of him. It appears from these books that the whole
time of his being a preacher was not more than eighteen months;
and it was only during this short time that these men became
acquainted with him. They make mention of him at the age of
twelve years, sitting, they say, among the Jewish doctors, asking
and answering them questions. As this was several years before
their acquaintance with him began, it is most probable they had
this anecdote from his parents. From this time there is no account of him for about sixteen years. Where he lived, or how
he employed himself during this interval, is not known. Most
probably he was working at his father's trade, which was that
of a carpenter. It does not appear that he had any school education, and the probability is that he could not write, for his
parents were extremely poor, as appears from their not being
able to pay for a bed when he was born.

It is somewhat curious that the three persons whose names
are the most universally recorded were of very obscure parentage. Moses was a foundling; Jesus Christ was born in a stable;
and Mohammed was a mule driver. The first and last of these
men were founders of different systems of religion; but Jesus
Christ founded no new system. He called men to the practice of
moral virtues and the belief of one God. The great trait in his
character is philanthropy.

The manner in which he was apprehended shows that he was
not much known at that time; and it shows also that the meet-
ings he then held with his followers were in secret; and that he
had given over or suspended preaching publicly. Judas could
not otherwise betray him than by giving information where he
was, and pointing him out to the officers that went to arrest
him; and the reason for employing and paying Judas to do this

could arise only from the cause already mentioned—that of his not being much known and living concealed.

The idea of his concealment not only agrees very ill with his reputed divinity, but associates with it something of pusillanimity; and being betrayed, or in other words, his being apprehended, on the information of one of his followers, shows that he did not intend to be apprehended, and consequently that he did not intend to be crucified.

The Christian mythologists tell us that Christ died for the sins of the world, and that he came on *purpose to die.* Would it not then have been the same if he had died of a fever or of the smallpox, of old age, or of anything else?

The declaratory sentence which, they say, was passed upon Adam, in case he eat of the apple, was not that *thou shalt surely be crucified,* but *thou shalt surely die*—the sentence of death, and not the manner of dying. Crucifixion, therefore, or any other particular manner of dying, made no part of the sentence that Adam was to suffer, and consequently, even upon their own tactics, it could make no part of the sentence that Christ was to suffer in the room of Adam. A fever would have done as well as the cross if there was any occasion for either.

The sentence of death, which they tell us was thus passed upon Adam, must either have meant dying naturally, that is, ceasing to live, or have meant what these mythologists call damnation; and consequently the act of dying on the part of Jesus Christ must, according to their system, apply as a prevention to one or other of these two *things* happening to Adam and to us.

That it does not prevent our dying is evident, because we all die; and if their accounts of longevity be true, men die faster since the crucifixion than before; and with respect to the second explanation (including with it the *natural death* of Jesus Christ as a substitute for the *eternal death or damnation of all mankind*), it is impertinently representing the Creator as coming off or revoking the sentence by a pun or a quibble upon the word "death." That manufacturer of quibbles, St. Paul, if he wrote the books that bear his name, has helped this quibble on by making another quibble upon the word "Adam." He makes there to be two Adams: the one who sins in fact, and suffers by proxy; the other who sins by proxy, and suffers in fact. A religion thus interlarded with quibble, subterfuge, and pun has a tendency to instruct its professors in the practice of these arts. They acquire the habit without being aware of the cause.

If Jesus Christ was the being which those mythologists tell us he was, and that he came into this world to *suffer,* which is a word they sometimes use instead of *die,* the only real suffering he could have endured would have been *to live.* His existence here was a state of exilement or transportation from Heaven and the way back to his original country was to die. In fine, everything in this strange system is the reverse of what it pretends to be. It is the reverse of truth, and I become so tired of examining into its inconsistencies and absurdities that I hasten to the conclusion of it in order to proceed to something better.

How much or what parts of the books called the New Testament were written by the persons whose names they bear is what we can know nothing of; neither are we certain in what language they were originally written. The matters they now contain may be classed under two heads—anecdote and epistolary correspondence.

The four books already mentioned, Matthew, Mark, Luke, and John, are altogether anecdotal. They relate events after they had taken place. They tell what Jesus Christ did and said, and what others did and said to him; and in several instances they relate the same event differently. Revelation is necessarily out of the question with respect to those books, not only because of the disagreement of the writers, but because revelation cannot be applied to the relating of facts by the person who saw them done, nor to the relating or recording of any discourse or conversation by those who heard it. The book called the Acts of the Apostles (an anonymous work) belongs also to the anecdotal part.

All the other parts of the New Testament, except the book of enigmas called the Revelations, are a collection of letters under the name of epistles, and the forgery of letters has been such a common practice in the world that the probability is at least equal whether they are genuine or forged. One thing, however, is much less equivocal, which is, that out of the matters contained in those books, together with the assistance of some old stories, the Church has set up a system of religion very contradictory to the character of the person whose name it bears. It has set up a religion of pomp and of revenue, in pretended imitation of a person whose life was humility and poverty.

The invention of purgatory and of the releasing of souls therefrom by prayers bought of the church with money; the selling of pardons, dispensations, and indulgences are revenue laws, without bearing that name or carrying that appearance. But the case nevertheless is that those things derive their origin from the paroxysm of the crucifixion and the theory deduced therefrom, which was that one person could stand in the place of another and could perform meritorious service for him. The probability, therefore, is that the whole theory or doctrine of what is called the redemption (which is said to have been accomplished by the act of one person in the room of another) was originally fabricated on purpose to bring forward and build all those secondary and pecuniary redemptions upon; and that the passages in the books upon which the idea or theory of redemption is built have been manufactured and fabricated for that purpose. Why are we to give this Church credit when she tells us that those books are genuine in every part, any more than we give her credit for everything else she has told us, or for the miracles she says she had performed? That she *could* fabricate writings is certain, because she could write; and the composition of the writings in question is of that kind that anybody might do it; and that she *did* fabricate them is not more inconsistent with probability than that she could tell us, as she has done, that she could and did work miracles.

Since then no external evidence can, at this long distance of time, be produced to prove whether the Church fabricated the doctrine called redemption or not (for such evidence, whether for or against, would be subject to the same suspicion of being fabricated), the case can only be referred to the internal evidence which the thing carries within itself; and this affords a very strong presumption of its being a fabrication. For the internal evidence is that the theory or doctrine of redemption has for its base an idea of pecuniary justice, and not that of moral justice.

If I owe a person money and cannot pay him, and he threatens to put me in prison, another person can take the debt upon himself and pay it for me; but if I have committed a crime, every circumstance of the case is changed; moral justice cannot take the innocent for the guilty, even if the innocent would offer itself. To suppose justice to do this is to destroy the principle of its existence, which is the thing itself; it is then no longer justice, it is indiscriminate revenge.

This single reflection will show that the doctrine of redemption is founded on a mere pecuniary idea corresponding to that of a debt which another person might pay; and as this pecuniary idea corresponds again with the system of second redemption, obtained through the means of money given to the Church for pardons, the probability is that the same persons fabricated both the one and the other of those theories; and that in truth there is no such thing as redemption—that it is fabulous, and that man stands in the same relative condition with his Maker as he ever did stand since man existed, and that it is his greatest consolation to think so.

Let him believe this, and he will live more consistently and morally than by any other system; it is by his being taught to contemplate himself as an outlaw, as an outcast, as a beggar, as a mumper, as one thrown, as it were, on a dunghill at an immense distance from his Creator, and who must make his approaches by creeping and cringing to intermediate beings, that he conceives either a contemptuous disregard for everything under the name of religion, or becomes indifferent, or turns what he calls devout. In the latter case, he consumes his life in grief, or the affectation of it; his prayers are reproaches; his humility is ingratitude; he calls himself a worm, and the fertile earth a dunghill; and all the blessings of life by the thankless name of vanities; he despises the choicest gift of God to man, the *gift of reason;* and having endeavored to force upon himself the belief of a system against which reason revolts, he ungratefully calls it "human reason," as if man could give reason to himself.

Yet, with all this strange appearance of humility and this contempt for human reason, he ventures into the boldest presumptions; he finds fault with everything; his selfishness is never satisfied; his ingratitude is never at an end. He takes on himself to direct the Almighty what to do, even in the government of the universe; he prays dictatorially; when it is sunshine, he prays for rain, and when it is rain, he prays for sunshine; he follows the same idea in everything that he prays for; for what is the amount of all his prayers but an attempt to make the Almighty change his mind and act otherwise than he does? It is as if he were to say: Thou knowest not so well as I.

But some, perhaps, will say: Are we to have no word of God —no revelation? I answer, Yes; there is a word of God; there is a revelation.

The word of God is the creation we behold: and it is in *this word,* which no human invention can counterfeit or alter, that God speaketh universally to man.

Human language is local and changeable, and is therefore incapable of being used as the means of unchangeable and universal information. The idea that God sent Jesus Christ to publish, as they say, the glad tidings to all nations, from one end of the earth to the other, is consistent only with the ignorance of those who knew nothing of the extent of the world, and who believed, as those world-saviors believed, and continued to believe for several centuries (and that in contradiction to the discoveries of philosophers and the experience of navigators) that the earth was flat like a trencher, and that a man might walk to the end of it.

But how was Jesus Christ to make anything known to all nations? He could speak but one language, which was Hebrew, and there are in the world several hundred languages. Scarcely any two nations speak the same language or understand each other; and as to translations, every man who knows anything of languages knows that it is impossible to translate from one language into another, not only without losing a great part of the original, but frequently mistaking the sense; and besides all this, the art of printing was wholly unknown at the time Christ lived.

It is always necessary that the means that are to accomplish any end be equal to the accomplishment of that end, or the end cannot be accomplished. It is in this that the difference between finite and infinite power and wisdom discovers itself. Man frequently fails in accomplishing his ends from a natural inability of the power to the purpose and frequently from the want of wisdom to apply power properly. But it is impossible for infinite power and wisdom to fail as man fails. The means it uses are always equal to the end; but human language, more especially as there is not a universal language, is incapable of being used as a universal means of unchangeable and uniform information, and therefore it is not the means that God uses in manifesting himself universally to man.

It is only in the *Creation* that all our ideas and conceptions of a *word of God* can unite. The Creation speaks a universal language, independently of human speech or human language, multiplied and various as they may be. It is an ever-existing original, which every man can read. It cannot be forged; it cannot be counterfeited; it cannot be lost; it cannot be altered; it cannot be suppressed. It does not depend upon the will of man whether it shall be published or not; it publishes itself from one end of the earth to the other. It preaches to all nations and to all worlds; and this *word of God* reveals to man all that is necessary for man to know of God.

Do we want to contemplate his power? We see it in the immensity of the Creation. Do we want to contemplate his wisdom? We see it in the unchangeable order by which the incomprehensible whole is governed. Do we want to contemplate his munificence? We see it in the abundance with which he fills the earth. Do we want to contemplate his mercy? We see it in his not withholding that abundance even from the unthankful. In fine, do we want to know what God is? Search not the book called the Scripture, which any human hand might make, but the Scripture called the Creation.

The only idea man can affix to the name of God is that of a *first cause,* the cause of all things. And incomprehensible and difficult as it is for a man to conceive what a first cause is, he arrives at the belief of it from the tenfold greater difficulty of disbelieving it. It is difficult beyond description to conceive that space can have no end; but it is more difficult to conceive an end. It is difficult beyond the power of man to conceive an eternal duration of what we call time; but it is more impossible to conceive a time when there shall be no time.

In like manner of reasoning, everything we behold carries in itself the internal evidence that it did not make itself. Every man is an evidence to himself that he did not make himself; neither could his father make himself, nor his grandfather, nor any of his race; neither could any tree, plant, or animal make itself; and it is the conviction arising from this evidence that carries us on, as it were, by necessity to the belief of a first cause eternally existing, of a nature totally different to any material existence we know of, and by the power of which all things exist; and this first cause man calls God.

It is only by the exercise of reason that man can discover God. Take away that reason and he would be incapable of understanding anything; and, in this case, it would be just as consistent to read even the book called the Bible to a horse as to a man. How, then, is it that those people pretend to reject reason?

Almost the only parts in the book called the Bible that convey to us any idea of God are some chapters in Job and the nineteenth Psalm; I recollect no other. Those parts are true *deistical* compositions, for they treat of the *Deity* through his works. They take the book of Creation as the word of God, they refer to no other book, and all the inferences they make are drawn from that volume.

I insert in this place the nineteenth Psalm, as paraphrased into English verse by Addison. I recollect not the prose, and where I write this I have not the opportunity of seeing it.

The spacious firmament on high,
With all the blue ethereal sky,
And spangled heavens, a shining frame,
Their great original proclaim.
The unwearied sun, from day to day,
Does his Creator's power display;
And publishes to every land
The work of an Almighty hand.

Soon as the evening shades prevail,
The moon takes up the wondrous tale,
And nightly to the list'ning earth
Repeats the story of her birth;
While all the stars that round her burn,
And all the planets, in their turn,
Confirm the tidings as they roll,
And spread the truth from pole to pole.

What though in solemn silence all
Move round this dark terrestrial ball?
What though no real voice, nor sound,
Amidst their radiant orbs be found?
In reason's ear they all rejoice
And utter forth a glorious voice,
Forever singing, as they shine,
The hand that made us is divine.

What more does man want to know than that the hand or
power that made these things is divine, is omnipotent? Let him
believe this with the force it is impossible to repel, if he permits
his reason to act, and his rule of moral life will follow, of course.

The allusions in Job have, all of them, the same tendency
with this Psalm—that of deducing or proving a truth that would
be otherwise unknown, from truths already known.

I recollect not enough of the passages in Job to insert them
correctly; but there is one occurs to me that is applicable to
the subject I am speaking upon: "Canst thou by searching find
out God? Canst thou find out the Almighty to perfection?"

I know not how the printers have pointed this passage, for I keep no Bible; but it contains two distinct questions that admit of distinct answers.

First—Canst thou by searching find out God? Yes; because in the first place, I know I did not make myself, and yet I have existence; and by *searching* into the nature of other things, I find out that no other thing could make itself; and yet millions of other things exist; therefore it is that I know, by positive conclusion resulting from this search, that there is a power superior to all those things, and that power is God.

Secondly—Canst thou find out the Almighty to *perfection?* No; not only because the power and wisdom He has manifested in the structure of the Creation that I behold is to me incomprehensible, but because even this manifestation, great as it is, is probably but a small display of that immensity of power and wisdom by which millions of other worlds, to me invisible by their distance, were created and continue to exist.

It is evident that both these questions were put to the reason of the person to whom they are supposed to have been addressed; and it is only by admitting the first question to be answered affirmatively that the second could follow. It would have been unnecessary and even absurd to have put a second question, more difficult than the first, if the first question had been answered negatively. The two questions have different objects: the first refers to the existence of God, the second to his attributes; reason can discover the one, but it falls infinitely short in discovering the whole of the other.

I recollect not a single passage in all the writings ascribed to the men called apostles that conveys any idea of what God is. Those writings are chiefly controversial; and the subject they dwell upon, that of a man dying in agony on a cross, is better suited to the gloomy genius of a monk in a cell, by whom it is not impossible they were written, than to any man breathing the open air of the Creation. The only passage that occurs to me that has any reference to the works of God, by which only his power and wisdom can be known, is related to have been spoken by Jesus Christ as a remedy against distrustful care.

"Behold the lilies of the field, they toil not, neither do they spin." This, however, is far inferior to the allusions in Job and in the nineteenth Psalm; but it is similar in idea, and the modesty of the imagery is correspondent to the modesty of the man.

As to the Christian system of faith, it appears to me as a species of atheism—a sort of religious denial of God. It professes to believe in a man rather than in God. It is a compound made up chiefly of Manism with but little Deism, and is as near to atheism as twilight is to darkness. It introduces between man and his Maker an opaque body, which it calls a redeemer, as the moon introduces her opaque self between the earth and the sun, and it produces by this means a religious, or an irreligious, eclipse of light. It has put the whole orbit of reason into shade.

The effect of this obscurity has been that of turning everything upside down and representing it in reverse, and among the revolutions it has thus magically produced, it has made a revolution in theology.

That which is now called natural philosophy, embracing the whole circle of science, of which astronomy occupies the chief place, is the study of the works of God and of the power and wisdom of God in his works, and is the true theology.

As to the theology that is now studied in its place, it is the study of human opinions and of human fancies *concerning* God. It is not the study of God himself in the works that he has made, but in the works or writings that man has made; and it is not among the least of the mischiefs that the Christian system has done to the world, that it has abandoned the original and beautiful system of theology, like a beautiful innocent, to distress and reproach, to make room for the hag of superstition.

The Book of Job and the nineteenth Psalm, which even the Church admits to be more ancient than the chronological order in which they stand in the book called the Bible, are theological orations conformable to the original system of theology. The internal evidence of those orations proves to a demonstration that the study and contemplation of the works of creation and of the power and wisdom of God revealed and manifested in those works made a great part in the religious devotion of the times in which they were written; and it was this devotional study and contemplation that led to the discovery of the principles upon which what are now called sciences are established; and it is to the discovery of these principles that almost all the arts that contribute to the convenience of human life owe their existence. Every principal art has some science for its parent, though the person who mechanically performs the work does not always, and but very seldom, perceive the connection.

It is a fraud of the Christian system to call the sciences "human invention"; it is only the application of them that is human. Every science has for its basis a system of principles as fixed and unalterable as those by which the universe is regulated and governed. Man cannot make principles, he can only discover them.

For example: every person who looks at an almanac sees an account when an eclipse will take place, and he sees also that it never fails to take place according to the account there given. This shows that man is acquainted with the laws by which the heavenly bodies move. But it would be something worse than ignorance were any Church on earth to say that those laws are a human invention. It would also be ignorance, or something worse, to say that the scientific principles by the aid of which man is enabled to calculate and foreknow when an eclipse will take place are a human invention. Man cannot invent a thing that is eternal and immutable; and the scientific principles he employs for this purpose must be, and are of necessity, as eternal and immutable as the laws by which the heavenly bodies move, or they could not be used as they are to ascertain the time when, and the manner how, an eclipse will take place.

The scientific principles that man employs to obtain the foreknowledge of an eclipse, or of anything else relating to the motion of the heavenly bodies, are contained chiefly in that part of science which is called trigonometry, or the properties of a triangle, which, when applied to the study of the heavenly bodies, is called astronomy; when applied to direct the course of a ship on the ocean, it is called navigation; when applied to the construction of figures drawn by rule and compass, it is called

Everything has an origin from God, man develops things from those principles.

THE AGE OF REASON 31

geometry; when applied to the construction of plans and edifices, it is called architecture; when applied to the measurement of any portion of the surface of the earth, it is called land surveying. In fine, it is the soul of science; it is an eternal truth; it contains the *mathematical demonstration* of which man speaks, and the extent of its uses is unknown.

It may be said that man can make or draw a triangle and, therefore, a triangle is a human invention.

But the triangle, when drawn, is no other than the image of the principle; it is a delineation to the eye, and from thence to the mind, of a principle that would otherwise be imperceptible. The triangle does not make the principle any more than a candle taken into a room that was dark makes the chairs and tables that before were invisible. All the properties of a triangle exist independently of the figure, and existed before any triangle was drawn or thought of by man. Man had no more to do in the formation of these properties or principles than he had to do in making the laws by which the heavenly bodies move; and therefore the one must have the same divine origin as the other.

In the same manner as it may be said that man can make a triangle, so also may it be said he can make the mechanical instrument called a lever; but the principle by which the lever acts is a thing distinct from the instrument, and would exist if the instrument did not; it attaches itself to the instrument after it is made; the instrument, therefore, cannot act otherwise than it does act; neither can all the efforts of human invention make it act otherwise—that which, in all such cases, man calls the *effect* is no other than the principle itself rendered perceptible to the senses.

Since, then, man cannot make principles, from whence did he gain a knowledge of them so as to be able to apply them, not only to things on earth, but to ascertain the motion of bodies so immensely distant from him as all the heavenly bodies are? From whence, I ask, *could* he gain that knowledge but from the study of the true theology?

It is the structure of the universe that has taught this knowledge to man. That structure is an ever-existing exhibition of every principle upon which every part of mathematical science is founded. The offspring of this science is mechanics, for mechanics is no other than the principles of science applied practically. The man who proportions the several parts of a mill uses the same scientific principles as if he had the power of constructing a universe; but as he cannot give to matter that invisible agency by which all the component parts of the immense machine of the universe have influence upon each other and act in motional unison together, without any apparent contact, and to which man has given the name of attraction, gravitation, and repulsion, he supplies the place of that agency by the humble imitation of teeth and cogs. All the parts of man's microcosm must visibly touch; but could he gain a knowledge of that agency so as to be able to apply it in practice, we might then say that another *canonical book* of the word of God had been discovered.

If man could alter the properties of the lever, so also could he alter the properties of the triangle, for a lever (taking that sort of lever which is called a steelyard, for the sake of explanation) forms, when in motion, a triangle. The line it descends from (one point of that line being in the fulcrum), the line it descends to, and the cord of the arc which the end of the lever describes in the air, are the three sides of a triangle. The other arm of the lever describes also a triangle; and the corresponding sides of those two triangles, calculated scientifically, or measured geometrically, and also the sines, tangents, and secants generated from the angles and geometrically measured, have the same proportions to each other as the different weights have that will balance each other on the lever, leaving the weight of the lever out of the case.

It may also be said that man can make a wheel and axis, that he can put wheels of different magnitudes together and produce a mill. Still the case comes back to the same point, which is, that he did not make the principle that gives the wheels those powers. That principle is as unalterable as in the former case, or rather it is the same principle under a different appearance to the eye.

The power that two wheels of different magnitudes have upon each other is in the same proportion as if the semidiameter of the two wheels were joined together and made into that kind of lever I have described, suspended at the part where the semi-diameters join, for the two wheels, scientifically considered, are no other than the two circles generated by the motion of the compound lever.

It is from the study of the true theology that all our knowledge of science is derived, and it is from that knowledge that all the arts have originated.

The Almighty Lecturer, by displaying the principles of science in the structure of the universe, has invited man to study and to imitation. It is as if He had said to the inhabitants of this globe that we call ours, "I have made an earth for man to dwell upon, and I have rendered the starry heavens visible to teach him science and the arts. He can now provide for his own comfort *and learn from my munificence to all to be kind to each other.*"

Of what use is it, unless it be to teach man something, that his eye is endowed with the power of beholding to an incomprehensible distance an immensity of worlds revolving in the ocean of space? Or of what use is it that this immensity of worlds is visible to man? What has man to do with the Pleiades, with Orion, with Sirius, with the star he calls the North Star, with the moving orbs he has named Saturn, Jupiter, Mars, Venus, and Mercury, if no uses are to follow from their being visible? A less power of vision would have been sufficient for man if the immensity he now possesses were given only to waste itself, as it were, on an immense desert of space glittering with shows.

It is only by contemplating what he calls the starry heavens as the book and school of science that he discovers any use in their being visible to him, or any advantage resulting from his immensity of vision. But when he contemplates the subject in this light, he sees an additional motive for saying that *nothing was made in vain;* for in vain would be this power of vision if it taught man nothing.

As the Christian system of faith has made a revolution in

theology, so also has it made a revolution in the state of learning. That which is now called learning was not learning originally. Learning does not consist, as the schools now make it consist, in the knowledge of languages, but in the knowledge of things to which language gives names.

The Greeks were a learned people, but learning with them did not consist in speaking Greek, any more than in a Roman's speaking Latin, or a Frenchman's speaking French, or an Englishman's speaking English. From what we know of the Greeks, it does not appear that they knew or studied any language but their own, and this was one cause of their becoming so learned; it afforded them more time to apply themselves to better studies. The schools of the Greeks were schools of science and philosophy, and not of languages; and it is in the knowledge of the things that science and philosophy teach that learning consists.

Almost all the scientific learning that now exists came to us from the Greeks or the people who spoke the Greek language. It, therefore, became necessary for the people of other nations who spoke a different language that some among them should learn the Greek language, in order that the learning the Greeks had might be made known in those nations by translating the Greek books of science and philosophy into the mother tongue of each nation.

The study, therefore, of the Greek language (and in the same manner for the Latin) was no other than the drudgery business of a linguist; and the language thus obtained was no other than the means, as it were the tools, employed to obtain the learning the Greeks had. It made no part of the learning itself, and was so distinct from it as to make it exceedingly probable that the persons who had studied Greek sufficiently to translate those works, such, for instance, as Euclid's *Elements,* did not understand any of the learning the works contained.

As there is now nothing new to be learned from the dead languages, all the useful books being already translated, the languages are become useless, and the time expended in teaching and learning them is wasted. So far as the study of languages

may contribute to the progress and communication of knowledge (for it has nothing to do with the *creation of* knowledge),
it is only in the living languages that new knowledge is to be
found; and certain it is that, in general, a youth will learn more
of a living language in one year than a dead language in seven,
and it is but seldom that the teacher knows much of it himself.
The difficulty of learning the dead languages does not arise
from any superior abstruseness in the languages themselves, but
in their *being dead,* and the pronunciation entirely lost. It
would be the same thing with any other language when it becomes dead. The best Greek linguist that now exists does not
understand Greek so well as a Grecian plowman did, or a
Grecian milkmaid; and the same for the Latin, compared with
a plowman or a milkmaid of the Romans; it would therefore be
advantageous to the state of learning to abolish the study of the
dead languages and to make learning consist, as it originally
did, in scientific knowledge.

The apology that is sometimes made for continuing to teach
the dead languages is that they are taught at a time when a child
is not capable of exerting any other mental faculty than that of
memory; but that is altogether erroneous. The human mind
has a natural disposition to scientific knowledge and to the
things connected with it. The first and favorite amusement of a
child, even before it begins to play, is that of imitating the works
of man. It builds houses with cards or sticks; it navigates the
little ocean of a bowl of water with a paper boat, or dams the
stream of a gutter and contrives something which it calls a mill;
and it interests itself in the fate of its works with a care that
resembles affection. It afterward goes to school, where its genius
is killed by the barren study of a dead language, and the philos-
opher is lost in the linguist.

But the apology that is now made for continuing to teach the
dead languages could not be the cause, at first, of cutting down
learning to the narrow and humble sphere of linguistry; the
cause, therefore, must be sought for elsewhere. In all researches
of this kind, the best evidence that can be produced is the in-

ternal evidence the thing carries with itself, and the evidence of circumstances that unite with it; both of which, in this case, are not difficult to be discovered.

Putting then aside, as a matter of distinct consideration, the outrage offered to the moral justice of God by supposing him to make the innocent suffer for the guilty, and also the loose morality and low contrivance of supposing him to change himself into the shape of a man in order to make an excuse to himself for not executing his supposed sentence upon Adam—putting, I say, those things aside as a matter of distinct consideration, it is certain that what is called the Christian system of faith, including in it the whimsical account of the creation—the strange story of Eve—the snake and the apple—the ambiguous idea of a man-god—the corporeal idea of the death of a god—the mythological idea of a family of gods, and the Christian system of arithmetic that three are one, and one is three, are all irreconcilable, not only to the divine gift of reason that God has given to man, but to the knowledge that man gains of the power and wisdom of God by the aid of the sciences and by studying the structure of the universe that God has made.

The setters-up, therefore, and the advocates of the Christian system of faith could not but foresee that the continually progressive knowledge that man would gain, by the aid of science, of the power and wisdom of God manifested in the structure of the universe and in all the works of Creation would militate against, and call into question, the truth of their system of faith; and therefore it became necessary to their purpose to cut learning down to a size less dangerous to their project, and this they effected by restricting the idea of learning to the dead study of dead languages.

They not only rejected the study of science out of the Christian schools, but they persecuted it, and it is only within about the last two centuries that the study has been revived. So late as 1610, Galileo, a Florentine, discovered and introduced the use of telescopes, and by applying them to observe the motions and appearances of the heavenly bodies afforded additional means for ascertaining the true structure of the universe. Instead of being esteemed for those discoveries, he was sentenced to renounce them, or the opinions resulting from them, as a damnable heresy. And, prior to that time, Vigilius was condemned to be burned for asserting the antipodes or, in other words, that the earth was a globe and habitable in every part where there was land; yet the truth of this is now too well known even to be told.

If the belief of errors not morally bad did no mischief, it would make no part of the moral duty of man to oppose and remove them. There was no moral ill in believing the earth was flat like a trencher, any more than there was moral virtue in believing that it was round like a globe; neither was there any moral ill in believing that the Creator made no other world than this, any more than there was moral virtue in believing that he made millions and that the infinity of space is filled with worlds. But when a system of religion is made to grow out of a supposed system of creation that is not true, and to unite itself therewith in a manner almost inseparable therefrom, the case assumes an entirely different ground. It is then that errors not morally bad become fraught with the same mischiefs as if they were. It is then that the truth, though otherwise indifferent itself, becomes an essential by becoming the criterion that either confirms by corresponding evidence, or denies by contradictory evidence, the reality of the religion itself. In this view of the case, it is the moral duty of man to obtain every possible evidence that the structure of the heavens or any other part of creation affords with respect to systems of religion. But this the supporters or partisans of the Christian system, as if dreading the result, incessantly opposed, and not only rejected the sciences but persecuted the professors. Had Newton or Descartes lived three or four hundred years ago and pursued their studies as they did, it is most probable they would not have lived to finish them; and had Franklin drawn lightning from the clouds at the same time, it would have been at the hazard of expiring for it in the flames.

Later times have laid all the blame upon the Goths and Vandals; but, however unwilling the partisans of the Christian system may be to believe or to acknowledge it, it is nevertheless true that the age of ignorance commenced with the Christian system. There was more knowledge in the world before that period than for many centuries afterward; and as to religious knowledge, the Christian system, as already said, was only another species of mythology, and the mythology to which it succeeded was a corruption of an ancient system of theism.[4]

It is owing to this long interregnum of science, *and to no other cause,* that we have now to look through a vast chasm of many hundred years to the respectable characters we call the ancients. Had the progression of knowledge gone on proportionably with that stock that before existed, that chasm would have been filled up with characters rising superior in knowledge to each other; and those ancients we now so much admire would have appeared respectably in the background of

[4] It is impossible for us now to know at what time the heathen mythology began; but it is certain, from the internal evidence that it carries, that it did not begin in the same state or condition in which it ended. All the gods of that mythology, except Saturn, were of modern invention. The supposed reign of Saturn was prior to that which is called the heathen mythology, and was so far a species of theism that it admitted the belief of only one God. Saturn is supposed to have abdicated the government in favor of his three sons and one daughter, Jupiter, Pluto, Neptune, and Juno; after this, thousands of other Gods and demigods were imaginarily created, and the calendar of gods increased as fast as the calendar of saints and the calendars of courts have increased since.

All the corruptions that have taken place in theology and in religion have been produced by admitting of what man calls "revealed religion." The mythologists pretended to more revealed religion than the Christians do. They had their oracles and their priests, who were supposed to receive and deliver the word of God verbally on almost all occasions.

Since then all corruptions, down from Moloch to modern predestinarianism, and the human sacrifices of the heathens to the Christian sacrifice of the Creator, have been produced by admitting of what is called "revealed religion"; the most effectual means to prevent all such evils and impositions is not to admit of any other revelation than that which is manifested in the book of creation, and to contemplate the creation as the only true and real word of God that ever did or ever will exist; and that everything else called the word of God is fable and imposition.

the scene. But the Christian system laid all waste; and if we take our stand about the beginning of the sixteenth century, we look back through that long chasm to the times of the ancients as over a vast sandy desert in which not a shrub appears to intercept the vision to the fertile hills beyond.

It is an inconsistency scarcely possible to be credited that anything should exist under the name of a religion that held it to be *irreligious* to study and contemplate the structure of the universe that God has made. But the fact is too well established to be denied. The event that served more than any other to break the first link in this long chain of despotic ignorance is that known by the name of the Reformation by Luther. From that time, though it does not appear to have made any part of the intention of Luther or of those who are called reformers, the sciences began to revive, and liberality, their natural associate, began to appear. This was the only public good the Reformation did; for with respect to religious good it might as well not have taken place. The mythology still continued the same, and a multiplicity of National Popes grew out of the downfall of the Pope of Christendom.

Having thus shown from the internal evidence of things the cause that produced a change in the state of learning, and the motive for substituting the study of the dead languages in the place of the sciences, I proceed, in addition to several observations already made in the former part of this work, to compare or rather to confront the evidence that the structure of the universe affords with the Christian system of religion; but, as I cannot begin this part better than by referring to the ideas that occurred to me at an early part of life, and which I doubt not have occurred in some degree to almost every person at one time or other, I shall state what those ideas were and add thereto such other matter as shall arise out of the subject, giving to the whole, by way of preface, a short introduction.

My father being of the Quaker profession, it was my good fortune to have an exceedingly good moral education and a tolerable stock of useful learning. Though I went to grammar

school,[5] I did not learn Latin, not only because I had no in-
clination to learn languages, but because of the objection the
Quakers have against the books in which the language is taught.
But this did not prevent me from being acquainted with the
subjects of all the Latin books used in the school.

The natural bent of my mind was to science. I had some turn,
and I believe some talent, for poetry; but this I rather repressed
than encouraged, as leading too much into the field of imagination. As soon as I was able I purchased a pair of globes and at-
tended the philosophical lectures of Martin and Ferguson, and
became afterward acquainted with Dr. Bevis, of the society
called the Royal Society, then living in the Temple, and an excellent astronomer.

I had no disposition for what is called politics. It presented
to my mind no other idea than as contained in the word Jockey-
ship. When, therefore, I turned my thoughts toward matters of
government, I had to form a system for myself that accorded
with the moral and philosophic principles in which I have been
educated. I saw, or at least I thought I saw, a vast scene open-
ing itself to the world in the affairs of America, and it appeared
to me that, unless the Americans changed the plan they were
pursuing with respect to the government of England and declared themselves independent, they would not only involve
themselves in a multiplicity of new difficulties, but shut out the
prospect that was then offering itself to mankind through their
means. It was from these motives that I published the work
known by the name of *Common Sense,* which is the first work
I ever did publish; and so far as I can judge of myself, I believe
I should never have been known in the world as an author, on
any subject whatever, had it not been for the affairs of America.
I wrote *Common Sense* the latter end of the year 1775, and published it the first of January, 1776. Independence was declared
the fourth of July following.

Any person who has made observations on the state and progress of the human mind by observing his own cannot but have

[5] The same school Thetford in Norfolk that the present Counselor
Mingay went to and under the same master.

observed that there are two distinct classes of what are called thoughts--those that we produce in ourselves by reflection and the act of thinking, and those that bolt into the mind of their own accord. I have always made it a rule to treat those voluntary visitors with civility, taking care to examine, as well as I was able, if they were worth entertaining, and it is from them I have acquired almost all the knowledge that I have. As to the learning that any person gains from school education, it serves only, like a small capital, to put him in a way of beginning learning for himself afterward. Every person of learning is finally his own teacher, the reason of which is that principles, being a distinct quality to circumstances, cannot be impressed upon the memory; their place of mental residence is the understanding and they are never so lasting as when they begin by conception. Thus much for the introductory part.

From the time I was capable of conceiving an idea and acting upon it by reflection, I either doubted the truth of the Christian system or thought it to be a strange affair; I scarcely knew which it was, but I well remember, when about seven or eight years of age, hearing a sermon read by a relation of mine who was a great devotee of the Church, upon the subject of what is called "redemption by the death of the Son of God." After the sermon was ended I went into the garden, and as I was going down the garden steps (for I perfectly recollect the spot), I revolted at the recollection of what I had heard, and thought to myself that it was making God Almighty act like a passionate man that killed his son when he could not revenge himself in any other way, and as I was sure a man would be hanged that did such a thing, I could not see for what purpose they preached such sermons. This was not one of that kind of thoughts that had anything in it of childish levity; it was to me a serious reflection, arising from the idea I had that God was too good to do such an action, and also too almighty to be under any necessity of doing it. I believe in the same manner at this moment; and I moreover believe that any system of religion that has anything in it that shocks the mind of a child cannot be a true system.

It seems as if parents of the Christian profession were ashamed to tell their children anything about the principles of their religion. They sometimes instruct them in morals and talk to them of the goodness of what they call Providence, for the Christian mythology has five deities—there is God the Father, God the Son, God the Holy Ghost, the God Providence, and the Goddess Nature. But the Christian story of God the Father putting his son to death, or employing people to do it (for that is the plain language of the story), cannot be told by a parent to a child; and to tell him that it was done to make mankind happier and better is making the story still worse—as if mankind could be improved by the example of murder; and to tell him that all this is a mystery is only making an excuse for the incredibility of it.

How different is this to the pure and simple profession of Deism! The true Deist has but one Deity, and his religion consists in contemplating the power, wisdom, and benignity of the Deity in his works, and in endeavoring to imitate him in everything moral, scientific, and mechanical.

The religion that approaches the nearest of all others to true Deism, in the moral and benign part thereof, is that professed by the Quakers; but they have contracted themselves too much, by leaving the works of God out of their system. Though I reverence their philanthropy, I cannot help smiling at the conceit, that if the taste of a Quaker could have been consulted at the creation, what a silent and drab-colored creation it would have been! Not a flower would have blossomed its gayeties, nor a bird been permitted to sing.

Quitting these reflections, I proceed to other matters. After I had made myself master of the use of the globes and of the orrery,[6] and conceived an idea of the infinity of space and the

---

[6] As this book may fall into the hands of persons who do not know what an orrery is, it is for their information I add this note, as the name gives no idea of the uses of the thing. The orrery has its name from the person who invented it. It is a machinery of clockwork, representing the universe in miniature, and in which the revolution of the earth round itself and round the sun, the revolution of the moon round the earth, the revolution of the

eternal divisibility of matter, and obtained at least a general knowledge of what is called natural philosophy, I began to compare or, as I have before said, to confront the eternal evidence those things afford with the Christian system of faith.

Though it is not a direct article of the Christian system that this world that we inhabit is the whole of the habitable creation, yet it is so worked up therewith, from what is called the Mosaic account of the Creation, the story of Eve and the apple, and the counterpart of that story, the death of the Son of God, that to believe otherwise, that is, to believe that God created a plurality of worlds, at least as numerous as what we call stars, renders the Christian system of faith at once little and ridiculous, and scatters it in the mind like feathers in the air. The two beliefs cannot be held together in the same mind, and he who thinks that he believes both has thought but little of either.

Though the belief of a plurality of worlds was familiar to the ancients, it is only within the last three centuries that the extent and dimensions of this globe that we inhabit have been ascertained. Several vessels, following the tract of the ocean, have sailed entirely round the world, as a man may march in a circle and come round by the contrary side of the circle to the spot he set out from. The circular dimensions of our world, in the widest part, as a man would measure the widest round of an apple or ball, is only twenty-five thousand and twenty English miles, reckoning sixty-nine miles and a half to an equatorial degree, and may be sailed round in the space of about three years.[7]

A world of this extent may, at first thought, appear to us to be great; but if we compare it with the immensity of space in

_____

planets round the sun, their relative distances from the sun, as the center of the whole system, their relative distances from each other, and their different magnitudes, are represented as they really exist in what we call the heavens.

[7] Allowing a ship to sail, on an average, three miles in an hour, she would sail entirely around the world in less than one year, if she could sail in a direct circle; but she is obliged to follow the course of the ocean.

which it is suspended, like a bubble or balloon in the air, it is infinitely less in proportion than the smallest grain of sand is to the size of the world or the finest particle of dew to the whole ocean, and is therefore but small; and, as will be hereafter shown, is only one of a system of worlds of which the universal creation is composed.

It is not difficult to gain some faint idea of the immensity of space in which this and all the other worlds are suspended if we follow a progression of ideas. When we think of the size or dimensions of a room, our ideas limit themselves to the walls, and there they stop; but when our eye or our imagination darts into space, that is, when it looks upward into what we call the open air, we cannot conceive any walls or boundaries it can have; and if for the sake of resting our ideas we suppose a boundary, the question immediately renews itself and asks, What is beyond that boundary? and in the same manner, What is beyond the next boundary? and so on till the fatigued imagination returns and says, *There is no end.* Certainly, then, the Creator was not pent for room when he made this world no larger than it is, and we have to seek the reason in something else.

If we take a survey of our own world, or rather of this of which the Creator has given us the use as our portion in the immense system of creation, we find every part of it—the earth, the waters, and the air that surrounds it—filled and, as it were, crowded with life, down from the largest animals that we know of to the smallest insects the naked eye can behold, and from thence to others still smaller and totally invisible without the assistance of the microscope. Every tree, every plant, every leaf, serves not only as a habitation but as a world to some numerous race, till animal existence becomes so exceedingly refined that the effluvia of a blade of grass would be food for thousands.

Since, then, no part of our earth is left unoccupied, why is it to be supposed that the immensity of space is a naked void lying in eternal waste? There is room for millions of worlds as large or larger than ours, and each of them millions of miles apart from each other.

Having now arrived at this point, if we carry our ideas only one thought further, we shall see, perhaps, the true reason, at least a very good reason, for our happiness, why the Creator, instead of making one immense world extending over an immense quantity of space, has preferred dividing that quantity of matter into several distinct and separate worlds, which we call planets, of which our earth is one. But before I explain my ideas upon this subject, it is necessary (not for the sake of those who already know, but for those who do not) to show what the system of the universe is.

That part of the universe that is called the solar system (meaning the system of worlds to which our earth belongs, and of which *sol*, or, in English language, the sun, is the center) consists, besides the sun, of six distinct orbs, or planets, or worlds, besides the secondary bodies called the satellites or moons, of which our earth has one that attends her in her annual revolution around the sun, in like manner as the other satellites or moons attend the planets or worlds to which they severally belong, as may be seen by the assistance of the telescope.

The sun is the center, round which those six worlds or planets revolve at different distances therefrom, and in circles concentric to each other. Each world keeps constantly in nearly the same track round the sun, and continues, at the same time, turning round itself in nearly an upright position, as a top turns round itself when it is spinning on the ground and leans a little sideways.

It is this leaning of the earth ($23\frac{1}{2}$ degrees) that occasions summer and winter, and the different length of days and nights. If the earth turned round itself in a position perpendicular to the plane or level of the circle it moves in around the sun, as a top turns round when it stands erect on the ground, the days and nights would be always of the same length, twelve hours day and twelve hours night, and the seasons would be uniformly the same throughout the year.

Every time that a planet (our earth, for example) turns round itself, it makes what we call day and night; and every time it goes entirely round the sun it makes what we call a year; consequently, our world turns three hundred and sixty-five times round itself in going once round the sun.[8]

The names that the ancients gave to those six worlds, and which are still called by the same names, are Mercury, Venus, this world we call ours, Mars, Jupiter, and Saturn. They appear larger to the eye than the stars, being many million miles nearer to our earth than any of the stars are. The planet Venus is that which is called the evening star, and sometimes the morning star, as she happens to set after or rise before the sun, which in either case is never more than three hours.

The sun, as before said, being the center, the planet or world nearest the sun is Mercury; his distance from the sun is thirty-four million miles, and he moves round in a circle always at that distance from the sun, as a top may be supposed to spin round in the track in which a horse goes in a mill. The second world is Venus; she is fifty-seven million miles distant from the sun, and, consequently, moves round in a circle much greater than that of Mercury. The third world is this that we inhabit, and which is eighty-eight million miles distant from the sun, and, consequently, moves round in a circle greater than that of Venus. The fourth world is Mars; he is distant from the sun one hundred and thirty-four million miles, and, consequently, moves round in a circle greater than that of our earth. The fifth is Jupiter; he is distant from the sun five hundred and fifty-seven million miles, and, consequently, moves round in a circle greater than that of Mars. The sixth world is Saturn; he is distant from the sun seven hundred and sixty-three million miles, and, consequently, moves round in a circle that surrounds the circles, or orbits, of all the other worlds or planets.

The space, therefore, in the air, or in the immensity of space, that our solar system takes up for the several worlds to perform their revolutions in round the sun is of the extent in a straight

[8] Those who supposed that the sun went round the earth every 24 hours made the same mistake in idea that a cook would do, in fact, that should make the fire go round the meat, instead of the meat turning round itself toward the fire.

line of the whole diameter of the orbit or circle in which Saturn moves round the sun, which, being double his distance from the sun, is fifteen hundred and twenty-six million miles and its circular extent is nearly five thousand million, and its globular content is almost three thousand five hundred million times three thousand five hundred million square miles.[9]

But this, immense as it is, is only one system of worlds. Beyond this, at a vast distance into space, far beyond all power of calculation, are the stars called the fixed stars. They are called fixed because they have no revolutionary motion as the six worlds or planets have that I have been describing. Those fixed stars continue always at the same distance from each other, and always in the same place, as the sun does in the center of our system. The probability, therefore, is that each of those fixed stars is also a sun, round which another system of worlds or planets, though too remote for us to discover, performs its revolutions, as our system of worlds does round our central sun.

By this easy progression of ideas, the immensity of space will appear to us to be filled with systems of worlds, and that no part of space lies at waste any more than any part of the globe of earth and water is left unoccupied.

Having thus endeavored to convey, in a familiar and easy manner, some idea of the structure of the universe, I return to

[9] If it should be asked how can man know these things? I have one plain answer to give, which is, that man knows how to calculate an eclipse, and also how to calculate to a minute of time when the planet Venus, in making her revolutions around the sun, will come in a straight line between our earth and the sun, and will appear to us about the size of a large pea passing across the face of the sun. This happens but twice in about a hundred years, at the distance of about eight years from each other, and has happened twice in our time, both of which were foreknown by calculation. It can also be known when they will happen again for a thousand years to come, or to any other portion of time. As, therefore, man could not be able to do these things if he did not understand the solar system, and the manner in which the revolutions of the several planets or worlds are performed, the fact of calculating an eclipse or a transit of Venus is a proof in point that the knowledge exists; and as to a few thousand, or even a few million, miles more or less it makes scarcely any sensible difference in such immense distances.

explain what I before alluded to, namely, the great benefits arising to man in consequence of the Creator having made a *plurality* of worlds, such as our system is, consisting of a central sun and six worlds, beside satellites, in preference to that of creating one world only of a vast extent.

It is an idea I have never lost sight of, that all our knowledge of science is derived from the revolutions (exhibited to our eye and from thence to our understanding) which those several planets or worlds of which our system is composed make in their circuit round the sun.

Had, then, the quantity of matter which these six worlds contain been blended into one solitary globe, the consequence to us would have been that either no revolutionary motion would have existed, or not a sufficiency of it to give to us the idea and the knowledge of science we now have; and it is from the sciences that all the mechanical arts that contribute so much to our earthly felicity and comfort are derived.

As, therefore, the Creator made nothing in vain, so also must it be believed that he organized the structure of the universe in the most advantageous manner for the benefit of man; and as we see, and from experience feel, the benefits we derive from the structure of the universe formed as it is, which benefits we should not have had the opportunity of enjoying if the structure, so far as relates to our system, had been a solitary globe— we can discover at least one reason why a *plurality* of worlds has been made, and that reason calls forth the devotional gratitude of man as well as his admiration.

But it is not to us, the inhabitants of this globe, only that the benefits arising from a plurality of worlds are limited. The inhabitants of each of the worlds of which our system is composed enjoy the same opportunities of knowledge as we do. They behold the revolutionary motions of our earth, as we behold theirs. All the planets revolve in sight of each other, and, therefore, the same universal school of science presents itself to all.

Neither does the knowledge stop here. The system of worlds next to us exhibits, in its revolutions, the same principles and school of science to the inhabitants of their system as our system does to us, and in like manner throughout the immensity of space.

Our ideas, not only of the almightiness of the Creator, but of his wisdom and his beneficence, become enlarged in proportion as we contemplate the extent and the structure of the universe. The solitary idea of a solitary world, rolling or at rest in the immense ocean of space, gives place to the cheerful idea of a society of worlds, so happily contrived as to administer, even by their motion, instruction to man. We see our own earth filled with abundance, but we forget to consider how much of that abundance is owing to the scientific knowledge the vast machinery of the universe has unfolded.

But in the midst of those reflections, what are we to think of the Christian system of faith that forms itself upon the idea of only one world, and that of no greater extent, as is before shown, than twenty-five thousand miles? An extent which a man walking at the rate of three miles an hour, for twelve hours in the day, could he keep on in a circular direction, would walk entirely round in less than two years. Alas! what is this to the mighty ocean of space and the almighty power of the Creator?

From whence, then, could arise the solitary and strange conceit that the Almighty, who had millions of worlds equally dependent on his protection, should quit the care of all the rest and come to die in our world, because, they say, one man and one woman had eaten an apple? And, on the other hand, are we to suppose that every world in the boundless creation had an Eve, an apple, a serpent, and a redeemer? In this case, the person who is irreverently called the Son of God, and sometimes God himself, would have nothing else to do than to travel from world to world, in an endless succession of deaths, with scarcely a momentary interval of life.

It has been by rejecting the evidence that the word or works of God in the creation afford to our senses, and the action of our reason upon that evidence, that so many wild and whimsical systems of faith and of religion have been fabricated and set up. There may be many systems of religion that, so far from being morally bad, are in many respects morally good; but there can be but *one* that is true; and that one necessarily must, as it ever will, be in all things consistent with the ever-existing word of God that we behold in his works. But such is the strange construction of the Christian system of faith that every evidence the Heavens afford to man either directly contradicts it or renders it absurd.

It is possible to believe, and I always feel pleasure in encouraging myself to believe it, that there have been men in the world who persuade themselves that what is called a "pious fraud" might, at least under particular circumstances, be productive of some good. But the fraud, being once established, could not afterward be explained, for it is with a pious fraud as with a bad action—it begets a calamitous necessity of going on.

The persons who first preached the Christian system of faith and in some measure combined it with the morality preached by Jesus Christ might persuade themselves that it was better than the heathen mythology that then prevailed. From the first preachers the fraud went on to the second, and to the third, till the idea of its being a pious fraud became lost in the belief of its being true; and that belief became again encouraged by the interests of those who made a livelihood by preaching it.

But though such a belief might by such means be rendered almost general among the laity, it is next to impossible to account for the continual persecution carried on by the Church, for several hundred years, against the sciences and against the professors of science if the Church had not some record or tradition that it was originally no other than a pious fraud, or did not foresee that it could not be maintained against the evidence that the structure of the universe afforded.

Having thus shown the irreconcilable inconsistencies between the real word of God existing in the universe and that which is called "the word of God," as shown to us in a printed book that any man might make, I proceed to speak of the three principal means that have been employed in all ages, and perhaps in all countries, to impose upon mankind.

Those three means are Mystery, Miracle, and Prophecy. The

two first are incompatible with true religion, and the third ought always to be suspected.

With respect to mystery, everything we behold is, in one sense, a mystery to us. Our own existence is a mystery; the whole vegetable world is a mystery. We cannot account how it is that an acorn, when put into the ground, is made to develop itself and become an oak. We know not how it is that the seed we sow unfolds and multiplies itself and returns to us such an abundant interest for so small a capital.

The fact, however, as distinct from the operating cause, is not a mystery, because we see it, and we know also the means we are to use, which is no other than putting the seed into the ground. We know, therefore, as much as is necessary for us to know; and that part of the operation that we do not know, and which, if we did, we could not perform, the Creator takes upon himself and performs it for us. We are, therefore, better off than if we had been let into the secret and left to do it for ourselves.

But though every created thing is, in this sense, a mystery, the word "mystery" cannot be applied to *moral truth* any more than obscurity can be applied to light. The God in whom we believe is a God of moral truth, and not a God of mystery or obscurity. Mystery is the antagonist of truth. It is a fog of human invention that obscures truth and represents it in distortion. Truth never envelops *itself* in mystery, and the mystery in which it is at any time enveloped is the work of its antagonist, and never of itself.

Religion, therefore, being the belief of a God and the practice of moral truth, cannot have connection with mystery. The belief of a God, so far from having anything of mystery in it, is of all beliefs the most easy, because it arises to us, as is before observed, out of necessity. And the practice of moral truth, or, in other words, a practical imitation of the moral goodness of God, is no other than our acting toward each other as he acts benignly toward all. We cannot *serve* God in the manner we serve those who cannot do without such service; and, therefore, the only idea we can have of serving God is that of contributing to the happiness of the living creation that God has made. This cannot be done by retiring ourselves from the society of the world and spending a recluse life in selfish devotion.

The very nature and design of religion, if I may so express it, prove, even to demonstration, that it must be free from everything of mystery, and unencumbered with everything that is mysterious. Religion, considered as a duty, is incumbent upon every living soul alike and, therefore, must be on a level with the understanding and comprehension of all. Man does not learn religion as he learns the secrets and mysteries of a trade. He learns the theory of religion by reflection. It arises out of the action of his own mind upon the things which he sees, or upon what he may happen to hear or to read, and the practice joins itself thereto.

When men, whether from policy or pious fraud, set up systems of religion incompatible with the word or works of God in the creation; and not only above, but repugnant to human comprehension, they were under the necessity of inventing or adopting a word that should serve as a bar to all questions, inquiries, and speculation. The word "mystery" answered this purpose, and thus it has happened that religion, which is in itself without mystery, has been corrupted into a fog of mysteries.

As *mystery* answered all general purposes, *miracle* followed as an occasional auxiliary. The former served to bewilder the mind, the latter to puzzle the senses. The one was the lingo, the other the legerdemain.

But before going further into this subject, it will be proper to inquire what is to be understood by a miracle.

In the same sense that everything may be said to be a mystery, so also may it be said that everything is a miracle, and that no one thing is a greater miracle than another. The elephant, though larger, is not a greater miracle than a mite, nor a mountain a greater miracle than an atom. To an almighty power it is no more difficult to make the one than the other, and no more difficult to make millions of worlds than to make one. Everything, therefore, is a miracle in one sense, whilst in the other sense there is no such thing as a miracle. It is a miracle when compared to our power and to our comprehension, it is not a miracle compared to the power that performs it; but as nothing in this description conveys the idea that is affixed to the word "miracle," it is necessary to carry the inquiry further.

Mankind have conceived to themselves certain laws by which what they call nature is supposed to act; and that a miracle is something contrary to the operation and effect of those laws; but unless we know the whole extent of those laws, and of what are commonly called the powers of nature, we are not able to judge whether anything that may appear to us wonderful or miraculous be within, or be beyond, or be contrary to, her natural power of acting.

The ascension of a man several miles high in the air would have everything in it that constitutes the idea of a miracle, if it were not known that a species of air can be generated, several times lighter than the common atmospheric air, and yet possess elasticity enough to prevent the balloon in which that light air is enclosed from being compressed into as many times less bulk by the common air that surrounds it. In like manner, extracting flames or sparks of fire from the human body, as visible as from a steel struck with a flint, and causing iron or steel to move without any visible agent, would also give the idea of a miracle if we were not acquainted with electricity and magnetism. So also would many other experiments in natural philosophy to those who are not acquainted with the subject. The restoring persons to life who are to appearance dead, as is practiced upon drowned persons, would also be a miracle if it were not known that animation is capable of being suspended without being extinct.

Besides these, there are performances by sleight-of-hand, and by persons acting in concert, that have a miraculous appearance which when known are thought nothing of. And besides these, there are mechanical and optical deceptions. There is now an exhibition in Paris of ghosts and specters which, though it is not imposed upon the spectators as a fact, has an astonishing appearance. As, therefore, we know not the extent to which either nature or art can go, there is no positive criterion to determine what a miracle is, and mankind, in giving credit to appearances under the idea of there being miracles are subject to be continually imposed upon.

Since, then, appearances are so capable of deceiving, and things not real have a strong resemblance to things that are, nothing can be more inconsistent than to suppose that the Almighty would make use of means such as are called miracles, that would subject the person who performed them to the suspicion of being an impostor, and the person who related them to be suspected of lying, and the doctrine intended to be supported thereby to be suspected as a fabulous invention.

Of all the modes of evidence that ever were invented to obtain belief to any system or opinion to which the name of religion has been given, that of miracle, however successful the imposition may have been, is the most inconsistent. For, in the first place, whenever recourse is had to show, for the purpose of procuring that belief (for a miracle, under any idea of the word, is a show), it implies a lameness or weakness in the doctrine that is preached. And, in the second place, it is degrading the Almighty into the character of a showman, playing tricks to amuse and make the people stare and wonder. It is also the most equivocal sort of evidence that can be set up; for the belief is not to depend upon the thing called a miracle, but upon the credit of the reporter who says that he saw it; and, therefore, the thing, were it true, would have no better chance of being believed than if it were a lie.

Suppose I were to say that when I sat down to write this book a hand presented itself in the air, took up the pen, and wrote every word that is herein written—would anybody believe me? Certainly, they would not. Would they believe me a whit the more if the thing had been a fact? Certainly, they would not. Since, then, a real miracle, were it to happen, would be subject to the same fate as the falsehood, the inconsistency becomes the greater of supposing the Almighty would make use of means that would not answer the purpose for which they were intended, even if they were real.

If we are to suppose a miracle to be something so entirely out of the course of what is called nature that she must go out of that course to accomplish it, and we see an account given of such miracle by the person who said he saw it, it raises a question in the mind very easily decided, which is, is it more probable that nature should go out of her course or that a man should tell a lie? We have never seen, in our time, nature go out of her course, but we have good reason to believe that millions of lies have been told in the same time; it is, therefore, at least millions to one that the reporter of a miracle tells a lie.

The story of the whale swallowing Jonah, though a whale is large enough to do it, borders greatly on the marvelous; but it would have approached nearer to the idea of a miracle if Jonah had swallowed the whale. In this, which may serve for all cases of miracles, the matter would decide itself, as before stated—namely, is it more probable that a man should have swallowed a whale or told a lie?

But suppose that Jonah had really swallowed the whale and gone with it in his belly to Nineveh, and, to convince the people that it was true, had cast it up in their sight, of the full length and size of a whale, would they not have believed him to have been the devil instead of a prophet? Or, if the whale had carried Jonah to Nineveh and cast him up in the same public manner, would they not have believed the whale to have been the devil and Jonah one of his imps?

The most extraordinary of all the things called miracles, related in the New Testament, is that of the devil flying away with Jesus Christ, and carrying him to the top of a high mountain, and to the top of the highest pinnacle of the temple, and showing him and promising to him *all the kingdoms of the world.* How happened it that he did not discover America, or is it only with kingdoms that his sooty highness has any interest?

I have too much respect for the moral character of Christ to believe that he told this whale of a miracle himself; neither is it easy to account for what purpose it could have been fabricated unless it were to impose upon the connoisseurs of miracles, as is sometimes practiced upon the connoisseurs of Queen Anne's farthings and collectors of relics and antiquities; or to render the belief of miracles ridiculous by outdoing miracles, as Don Quixote outdid chivalry; or to embarrass the belief of miracles by making it doubtful by what power, whether of God or of the devil, anything called a miracle was performed. It requires, however, a great deal of faith in the devil to believe this miracle.

In every point of view in which those things called miracles can be placed and considered, the reality of them is improbable and their existence unnecessary. They would not, as before observed, answer any useful purpose, even if they were true; for it is more difficult to obtain belief to a miracle than to a principle evidently moral without any miracle. Moral principle speaks universally for itself. Miracle could be but a thing of the moment and seen but by a few; after this it requires a transfer of faith from God to man to believe a miracle upon man's report. Instead, therefore, of admitting the recitals of miracles as evidences of any system of religion being true, they ought to be considered as symptoms of its being fabulous. It is necessary to the full and upright character of truth that it rejects the crutch, and it is consistent with the character of fable to seek the aid that truth rejects. Thus much for mystery and miracle.

As mystery and miracle took charge of the past and the present, prophecy took charge of the future and rounded the tenses of faith. It was not sufficient to know what had been done, but what would be done. The supposed prophet was the supposed historian of times to come; and if he happened, in shooting with a long bow of a thousand years, to strike within a thousand miles of a mark, the ingenuity of posterity could make it point-blank; and if he happened to be directly wrong, it was only to suppose, as in the case of Jonah and Nineveh, that God had repented himself and changed his mind. What a fool do fabulous systems make of man!

It has been shown in a former part of this work that the original meaning of the words "prophet" and "prophesying" has been changed, and that a prophet, in the sense of the word as now used, is a creature of modern invention; and it is owing to this change in the meaning of the words that the flights and metaphors of the Jewish poets, and phrases and expressions now rendered obscure by our not being acquainted with the local circumstances to which they applied at the time they were used, have been erected into prophecies and made to bend to explanations at the will and whimsical conceits of sectaries, expounders, and commentators. Everything unintelligible was prophetical, and everything insignificant was typical. A blunder would have served for a prophecy, and a dishclout for a type.

If by a prophet we are to suppose a man to whom the Almighty communicated some event that would take place in future, either there were such men or there were not. If there were, it is consistent to believe that the event so communicated would be told in terms that could be understood, and not related in such a loose and obscure manner as to be out of the comprehension of those that heard it, and so equivocal as to fit almost any circumstance that may happen afterward. It is conceiving very irreverently of the Almighty to suppose that he would deal in this jesting manner with mankind, yet all the things called prophecies in the book called the Bible come under this description.

But it is with prophecy as it is with miracle—it could not answer the purpose even if it were real. Those to whom a prophecy should be told could not tell whether the man prophesied or lied, or whether it had been revealed to him, or whether he conceited it; and if the thing that he prophesied, or intended to prophesy, should happen, or something like it, among the multitude of things that are daily happening, nobody could again know whether he foreknew it or guessed at it, or whether it was accidental. A prophet, therefore, is a character useless and unnecessary; and the safe side of the case is to guard against being imposed upon by not giving credit to such relations.

Upon the whole, mystery, miracle, and prophecy are appendages that belong to fabulous and not to true religion. They are the means by which so many *Lo, heres!* and *Lo, theres!* have been spread about the world and religion been made into a trade. The success of one impostor gave encouragement to another, and the quieting salvo of doing *some good* by keeping up a *pious fraud* protected them from remorse.

Having now extended the subject to a greater length than I first intended, I shall bring it to a close by abstracting a summary from the whole.

First—That the idea or belief of a word of God existing in print, or in writing, or in speech is inconsistent in itself for reasons already assigned. These reasons, among many others, are the want of a universal language; the mutability of language; the errors to which translations are subject; the possibility of totally suppressing such a word; the probability of altering it or of fabricating the whole and imposing it upon the world.

Secondly—That the Creation we behold is the real and ever-existing word of God in which we cannot be deceived. It proclaims his power, it demonstrates his wisdom, it manifests his goodness and beneficence.

Thirdly—That the moral duty of man consists in imitating the moral goodness and beneficence of God, manifested in the creation toward all his creatures. That seeing, as we daily do, the goodness of God to all men, it is an example calling upon all men to practice the same toward each other; and, consequently, that everything of persecution and revenge between man and man, and everything of cruelty to animals, is a violation of moral duty.

I trouble not myself about the manner of future existence. I content myself with believing, even to positive conviction, that the Power that gave me existence is able to continue it, in any form and manner he pleases, either with or without this body; and it appears more probable to me that I shall continue to exist hereafter than that I should have had existence, as I now have, before that existence began.

It is certain that in one point all nations of the earth and all religions agree—all believe in a God; the things in which they

disagree are the redundancies annexed to that belief; and, therefore, if ever a universal religion should prevail, it will not be by
believing anything new, but in getting rid of redundancies
and believing as man believed at first. Adam, if ever there were
such a man, was created a Deist; but in the meantime, let every
man follow, as he has a right to do, the religion and the worship
he prefers.